Diversity, Values, Professionalism, or Favoritism Racism

Diversity, Values, Professionalism,or Favoritism Racism

◆

African Americans & Other Minorities In The Work Force

Daniel Vincent Pierce

iUniverse, Inc.

New York Lincoln Shanghai

Diversity, Values, Professionalism,or Favoritism Racism
African Americans & Other Minorities In The Work Force

iUniverse books may be ordered through booksellers or by contacting:

iUniverse
2021 Pine Lake Road, Suite 100
Lincoln, NE 68512
www.iuniverse.com
1-800-Authors (1-800-288-4677)

Because of the dynamic nature of the Internet, any Web addresses or links contained in this book may have changed since publication and may no longer be valid.

The views expressed in this work are solely those of the author and do not necessarily reflect the views of the publisher, and the publisher hereby disclaims any responsibility for them.

ISBN: 978-0-595-47122-5 (pbk)
ISBN: 978-0-595-91402-9 (ebk)

Printed in the United States of America

"People make businesses or organizations prosper, and people ultimately decide whether these businesses or organizations stay in business because of the way they do their job." Diversity, Values, Professionalism or Favoritism, Racism whether or not people want to believe it in the work force does exist and it makes it difficult when African Americans and other minorities are the people that have to take the brunt end of this which happens to be Favoritism, Racism. The President of the United States and his cabinet, the individuals that write the laws in the Senate, and the justices that sit on the Supreme Court are the men that make the decisions that affect not only the lives of African Americans and other minorities but the lives of every citizen here in the United States as well are predominately white and male. A majority of the businesses and organizations here in the US large and small hire a majority of African Americans and other minorities to work for them, and in a majority of these cases the decisions that are made that affect the lives of these employees are made by men predominately white. How can equality and fairness on the job exist for African Americans and other minorities when the person or persons in charge who are predominately white and male have the option and or the power to make decisions that will keep an individual or individuals of color or other minorities from advancing to better their career and achieve their ultimate goal of success. Here in the United States in our federal government and a majority of businesses and organizations, African Americans and other minorities even though we have pride, integrity, efficiency, resourcefulness, courtesy and excellence and that is something that no one can take away from us as individuals, have concerns and issues with our federal government law makers and the laws that these group of individuals have passed to supposedly give us equal rights in our place of employment. I say this because of who we are and the type of positions some of us have at our jobs because, in some instances depending on the type of work we are doing unfortunately we get knocked down and left behind to many times. To me it seems as though even with the laws that have been passed and some progress that has been made to move forward, African Americans and other minorities still in some cases don't get the respect for the knowledge and skills that we have gained as individuals to do the type jobs that we are capable of doing.

As I'm sitting here putting together my ideas and thoughts to write this book a lot of things are going thru my mind but, one of the most important things that comes to mind right away is the fact that I'm an African American male and in today's society whether its in the work force or just my everyday life in general I have to fight to get respect because of the color of my skin and as a human being. I started talking to people, taking notes, and doing research for this book in early 2006, as I put what I consider to be the finishing touches on a subject that shouldn't even exist but does its now mid 2007 and I hoping once this book is read that a fire will be lit and just human beings period wont ever let it go out until everyone no matter the color of their skin receives equality and justice in this country.

There are some changes in our present day society going on that we need to keep eyes and ears open about starting with, the Presidential election coming in November of 2008 and check this out, even though a majority of the candidates are predominately white and male not only is diversity a part of the picture but the front runners and maybe the next President of the United States could be an African American male or a white female. Another point that should be mentioned is, in the previous year of 2006 a lot of political office positions held by long time politicians in those offices changed hands and fresh faces were voted in so with these changes, African Americans and other minorities not only in their everyday lives in general but in the workforce as well has a new voice to hear their concerns and issues and hopefully some type of change for the better should come about.

As we look at the positive you know there is always some type of negative that pops up in our face and once again lets us see that in this society every time we take one step forward an obstacle stands in our way to make us take two steps back. How about this, the 2006, 2007 women's college basketball season ended and we as African Americans and other minorities and just as a society in general had to deal with a white individual like Don Imus and his insensitive comments about a group of African American females that played basketball at a prestigious University. These comments drew the anger of I would think every decent human being in this country and once again lets us know that no matter how much we want to say that these type of words and this type of attitude is far and few away, it's right here in our back yard. As an African American male and a minority I know life in general is tough at times and I know at times things can be unbearable, I can't speak for every African American male or for that fact other minorities but I'd like to plant this thought in your mind and that is, don't give up, don't quit, keep a positive attitude and let the past stay behind you and look forward to what should be a lot of success and happiness in the future.

Diversity: Not looking at someone as a U.S. Citizen or not, man or woman, black or white, young or old but, just looking at someone as a human being, a person, the color of someone's skin or whether they are young or old shouldn't make a difference as long as they can do the job they are asked to do.

Values: Employees want to do their job, they want to express their opinions about their job to make it better, and in most cases safe and reliable for them to work in.

Professionalism: Working for pay is important because this is how people plan their lives, working in a profession no matter what it is, integrity and pride should be the main focus, the main goal, and the number one priority on the job.

Pride Integrity Efficiency Resourcefulness Courtesy Excellence

Pride: Do your job and do it well, don't walk away from your job saying I should have done this or that or next time I'll make sure I do the job right, do your job the way it should be done all the time.

Integrity: Be honest with yourself and your fellow employees don't do anything that would jeopardize your job or your fellow employee's job by doing something dishonest at work.

Efficiency: At work be adequate in your performance capable and competent and give a relatively high output on the job.

Resourcefulness: At work use any source of aid or support and be clever in finding and utilizing resources to do your job.

Courtesy: Come to work and be kind and show thoughtful behavior toward your fellow employees.

Excellence: When you come to work be remarkably good, go beyond required expectations, stand out and be recognized.

The Vision of Diversity Values and Professionalism

Diversity, Values, and Professionalism should be the focus, the main goal to keep our country operating effectively and efficiently and to give the citizens of the United States a fair and equal opportunity for employment.

The Mission of Diversity Values and Professionalism

To provide a healthy and safe work environment for employees and for the people in the communities that businesses and organizations are a part of, and to improve the environment of the community by providing Diversity, Values, and Professionalism thru employees.

A Statement of Integrity for Diversity Values and Professionalism

Pride, Integrity, Efficiency, Resourcefulness, Courtesy, Excellence, these are unselfish words that businesses and organizations should stand for and adhere to and every employee that is a part of a business or an organization should be unselfish and comply with these words without question or hesitation.

Diversity Values Professionalism

Or

Favoritism Racism

African Americans and Other Minorities

In The Work Force

This is not going to be a book about a lot of numbers, it's definitely not going to be a he said she said, and check this out, it's not even going to be about sex, lies, and video tapes sorry if your disappointed but, I'm going to tell you that as you continue to read some interesting and what I think some never ending conversational topics will be brought to your attention if you don't already know or realize them. I live in the Washington, D.C. metropolitan area and because of some issues that are going on at my present job that affect me and other African Americans and other minorities as well, we personally have to deal with these issues at this company we work for, and oh by the way not only that but, in some cases trying to advance into a position in management seems to be an even bigger issue. This is one of the reasons that I decided to write this book and as you continue to read whether you're an African American or another minority just imagine yourself in this type of position. Now for any employee that is trying to move into a leadership position in their company management is the next step up and in some cases it's a smooth transition and in other cases it's a difficult one for a number of reasons. In my case as well as other African Americans and other minorities at my present job and some African Americans and other minorities that I've talked to that work at other jobs in the Washington, D. C. metropolitan area, it is a difficult transition in a lot of cases. I'm talking about city government offices, state government offices, federal government offices, and privately owned businesses and companies, it has been a difficult transition to make because more than half of the individuals told me that instead of using the diversity of people that work for their company, taking under consideration the value of the employees that have in most cases been working for the company for a long period of time and not only that, looking at the professionalism that the employees are using to do their jobs at these companies. Instead, favoritism because some employees are more likeable than others and racism simply because someone is white, and that takes place in most instances because the person or persons that make the decisions about who gets promoted or not are predominately white and predominately male. The company that I work for in the department and the section that I work in the person that makes the decision about who gets a position in management and who doesn't is made by a white male individual. Now check this out, for the African Americans and other minorities that I've talked to on my job and others that I have talked to that work on jobs in this metropolitan area, the majority of them have said for some of the same reasons this is why they are having a difficult time making the transition from employee to management. The decisions that are made on a majority of jobs are made by predominately white predominately male individuals and these decisions affect in a lot of cases the education, lives and well-being of not only African Americans and other minorities but everyone that works on the job as well. At the company I work for the people in charge are predominately white and predominately male and a lot of the individuals that make the decisions that affect everyone that works for this company are predominately white and predominately male. It just seems to me that after talking to other African Americans and other minorities that this is the norm in a lot of companies in this metropolitan area to have predominately white and predominately male individuals making decisions that affect the people that work for these companies.

Talking to African Americans and other minorities in this Washington, D. C. metropolitan area about diversity, values, professionalism and favoritism, racism in the work force, I've done some research on the subject of how some businesses, companies or organizations what ever word you want to use is set up as far as the individuals in charge and how decisions that they make affect the health and welfare and ultimately the lives that some employees would like to live. Not only minority employees have to deal with the decisions that are made but the majority of it's employees as well, basically it comes down to the fact that the individual or individuals are predominately white and predominately male. I'd like to share with you what I've researched and after reading decide for yourself if you don't already have a clue about what is going on in our workforce and in our society as well and talk to your friends, neighbors and fellow co-workers because, these are important issues to not only me but to everyone whether you are an African American or a minority or just a human being, and this is another reason I choose this particular topic to write about.

Let me start you off with some food for thought, for to long in the past and right up to this present day some progress has been made to strengthen some positions that African Americans and other minorities have in our society but, after reading my book you decide for yourself if some of the positions we have are to satisfy us and make it seem as though we have advanced and are moving in the right direction or is it just a smoke screen to allow us to be put into certain positions to keep us happy so we won't make a lot of noise? Here's something else for you to think about, "How can we as African Americans and other minorities count on anybody to help us along in our career paths or our everyday lives when the obstacles of favoritism and racism literally stands in the way of us getting ahead."

Diversity, Values, Professionalism or Favoritism, Racism these are some powerful words that mean a lot to someone that's trying to make a decent living for themselves unfortunately, some people could care less about these words and try to put on a show to let you think they do when in reality they really don't. As African Americans and other minorities some of us get lucky and catch a break and get that position that we want and live the kind of lifestyle we want to live. In most cases though let's be real, the majority of us have to work hard hope for the best and maybe that break will come our way so, as African Americans and other minorities we fall into a category all our own, and that is the category of hope and pray. We hope that the job we're trying to get comes along and we're right there to jump on it, then after we get the job, we pray that nothing happens that will cause us to loose it. As African Americans and other minorities reality slaps us in the face all to often and to much and unfortunately as much as some things have gotten better for us, when we think that we are moving forward, the time is here and there's no stopping us now, we get slapped in the face again.

We are a multi cultural society, and in our society every man and woman is different, their concerns, issues, and opinions about what they believe in are different, and as a multi cultural society we should be able to agree to disagree about our differences but at times we can't. Diversity in our society and at work is what makes men and women different and how they view things make them different as well. Values in our society and on the job are what men and women value and believe in and that makes an even bigger difference as well. Professionalism in our society and as far as doing a job is concerned there is no difference because both men and women want time and effort put into what ever type of work is being done and they want it done in a professional manor. Favoritism in our society and at work basically is someone that is preferred or popular to people in certain positions that matter and that can make a difference to help them to move along and further their career. Racism in our society and on the job basically is showing prejudice against certain people and that is really the biggest obstacle that a lot of us as African Americans and other minorities have to face.

As you continue to read on here are some things that affect us as African Americans and other minorities and concerns and issues of what I believe evolves around Diversity, Values, Professionalism or Favoritism, Racism. Things that happen in our everyday lives that basically affect us in some kind of way, shape or form, and remember because sometimes we forget that in our society and in the work force as African Americans and other minorities it's not always how much education, qualifications, and skills we have along with the amount of time we may have on a job but, it sometimes comes down to who you know and what you know. If this is the case think about it, is it Diversity, Values, Professionalism or Favoritism, Racism.

Remember this, "People make businesses or organizations prosper, and people ultimately decide whether these businesses or organizations stay in business because of the way they do their job."

Today everyone that is old enough and able to work goes out to find a job that they are capable of doing, in most cases the company that they decides to work for may not be their first choice but, it may be the only choice they have at the time. Everyone doesn't go to college and everyone doesn't get the proper education or job skills to do the type of work they want to do and in most cases because of this some people will take a job doing what ever they can just to make a living to provide for themselves or if they have a family to provide for themselves and their family as well. Should it make a difference whether someone has the proper education and skills depending on the type of job they want to do or already working on, or should they have the proper education and skills for the job they are doing, in a lot of cases it makes a big difference. African Americans and other minorities in some instances on a job whether they have the education and skills or not are treated sometimes like they are second class citizens. In some cases increases in salaries are held up or denied, promotions and increases in salary are held up and denied, and in some cases both salary increases and promotions are held up and denied. Issues like this are frustrating to us as African Americans and other minorities that fall into this category because we feel as though we are being singled out and are not given a fair chance to prove what we can or can not do on our jobs.

Diversity, Values, and Professionalism and not Favoritism, Racism are important and should be the focus in our society and most importantly in our work force so, I ask you while reading these following statements think about what I'm saying.

Not looking at someone on the job as an African American or another minority or not, U.S. Citizen or not, man or woman, young or old but, just looking at someone as a human being, a person, whether he or she is young or old, black or white, or even if they are a U.S. Citizen or not shouldn't make a difference as long as they can do the job they are asked to do.

As an employee you want to do your job, you want to be able to express your opinion about the work that you do to make it better, and in most cases safe and reliable for you to work in.

Working for pay is important because this is how you plan your life, and working in a profession no matter what it is, integrity and pride should be a priority.

Let me just say that whether you are an employee or an employer in a business or an organization I think you should go to work with a good attitude, don't take the issues that are happening at home or even in your personal life to work with you. It's not fair to your employees or your fellow co-workers, the job that you have to do, or even where you work at, leave your issues behind and don't let the stress and strain if there is any control you at work. Sometimes personal issues can take over someone's life so bad that the out come can turn out to be catastrophic and in some cases the innocent bystanders are fellow co-workers or other innocent people that just happen to be in the way at that time. Let's not forget that everyone has personal issues it's just that some people can keep them under control better than others.

As African Americans and other minorities pride, integrity, efficiency, resourcefulness, courtesy, and excellence I think is not only a part of us as human beings but also as we go about our everyday lives something that no one can ever take away form us because we are special and we do stand out and believe it or not we aren't going anywhere anytime soon.

Just going to work is a task in it self but unless there is another way legally in this society to make a living this is what we have to do everyday of our lives until we become fortunate enough or happen to run into some luck where we don't have to work anymore so, as an African American and a minority here's some general advise good or bad however you want to use it for everyone that has a job to think about when you go to work.

Do your job and do it well, don't walk away from your job saying I should have done this or that or next time I'll make sure I do the job right, do your job the way it should be done all the time.

Be honest with yourself and your fellow employees don't do anything that would jeopardize your job or your fellow employee's job by doing something dishonest at work.

Be adequate in your performance capable and competent and give a relatively high output on the job.

Use any source of aid or support, and be clever in finding and utilizing resources to do your job.

Come to work and be kind and show thoughtful behavior toward your fellow employees.

When you come to work be remarkably good, go beyond required expectations, stand out and be recognized.

Now after what you've just read ask yourself if you have a job or you are the head of a company, as an employee when I go to work am I doing any or all of this, and as the head of a company do I operate this way. Changing yourself and your attitude as an employee which I know is tough because of some of the things you may have to deal with, and as an employer to keep things running the way you would like may be difficult at times as well, I think changing yourself and your attitude as an employee and as an employer could possibly make a big difference.

Diversity Values Professionalism or Favoritism, Racism, do you have to deal with this at work, is any or all of this going on at your job, lets just say in some cases it could be, in others it might be, and yet in others it is. There are some companies out there that Diversity Values and Professionalism and not Favoritism, Racism apply in every case and the employees that work for these companies like working for them. We as African Americans and even other minorities in the United States need the example of Diversity Values and Professionalism and not Favoritism, Racism set by our United States government.

To give you an example of what I'm talking about, The President of The United States George Bush and the cabinet that he has chosen to make the decisions that affect the lives of not only African Americans and other minorities but every citizen in the United States now get this, the people he has chosen to serve in his cabinet is predominately white and predominately male. I'm asking this question, were the people chosen to serve in this cabinet made by looking at the Diversity, Values and the Professionalism needed to do the type of work that is asked to be done to help this country move in the right direction or, were these people chosen out of Favoritism, Racism because they are predominately male and predominately white and their the one's that the President likes?

I started writing this book in January of 2006 and during this year there were local, state and federal elections, these elections once they were over would determine who stays and who goes in political offices around the country. Will the outcome of these elections affect the concerns and issues of African Americans and other minorities, it most certainly will and not only that, we as African Americans and other minorities have to look at the most important fact in general, will there be changes made or will things just remain the same, I guess we'll just have to wait and see.

As I watch the news on television and I read the newspaper it seems to me that the concerns and issues of some United States citizens, period, seem to be falling on death ears in our White House Administration. This administration in the minds of some people don't seem to value the people and their property here in the United States as they do in a foreign land, and the time that it is going to take to get there lives and their property back together where they can reasonably be comfortable and make a living for themselves. As professionals in the jobs that are being held in the White House and this administration why is it that so much finger pointing, misinformation, and in some cases what seems to be deception being given to the American public?

This administration has done so much to help people get their property and lives back together again and also what seems to be an undetermined time frame to do all of this in foreign countries but get this, here in the United States there are citizens that need to get their property and their lives back together and it is going to take more than a month, a year, two years, five years, it's going to take years to get back to the way they were, and just maybe things will never get back to the way they use to be. These U S citizens are being given ultimatums, deadlines and being told don't worry you will be taken care of, I'm talking about the victims of Hurricane Katrina. Unfortunately the government is making it seem like everything is going to be ok but the people that survived Hurricane Katrina have to go on living and don't see things that way. It's been said by some people that devastation and disparity can be overcome with faith and prayer, it makes it tough when you have to deal with obstacles that are standing in your way. The obstacles that I'm referring to is, the U S government and the slow response time, deadlines and ultimatums to people that need help and it seems as though help is taking its time about coming their way.

This country has seen in the last five years two devastating tragedies that we will always remember and most certainly will never forget, I talking about that horrible day September 11, 2001, and the catastrophe of Hurricane Katrina. These two events shocked not only the people here in the US but also, millions of people around the world. I would think it has to be hard to go on with your everyday life if you had loved one's that lost their lives on September 11, 2001. To be reminded about that day on motion picture and television screens, to have the news media when that date comes around and on that date showing pictures of all of the devastation that occurred has to be heart breaking. We will never forget what happened but certainly I don't think that every time that date comes around we need to be shown those pictures of devastation and destruction to remind us of that horrible event.

The tragedy of what we now refer to as 9/11 when it happened I know was tough for everyone including African Americans and other minorities but this is what I'm saying, in a majority of the depictions that we see about this event no African Americans or any other minority is even talked about. In the movie World Trade Center, evidently not to much research was done because an African American by the name of Jason Thomas was one of the individuals that helped in a rescue mission of some people that were trapped in some of the collapsed building debris. He wasn't even depicted in the movie as such; unfortunately he was depicted as non African American and after the movie was finished and this fact was found out steps was taken to acknowledge him and to let people know that he helped in this rescue mission. This may seem trivial to some people but in any instance all I'm trying to say is that a lot of African Americans and other minorities lost their lives and their families and friends as well and feel just as much pain and just as much suffering about what happened on that day as well but for some reason, just the predominately white tragedies about what happened are being shown and talked about so it just makes me wonder why is only one side of this story being told.

As far as Hurricane Katrina is concerned no we can't forget, yes we need a constant reminder, and yes this tragedy not only took the lives of people and didn't care if you were black, white or what ever to this day people that survived this event are still waiting and wondering when help for them will be arriving. The President of the United States and the federal government are both saying help is coming, you are going to be taken care of, don't worry we haven't forgotten about you well, unless you just haven't been keeping up with what's been happening since Katrina struck at the time that I'm writing this book almost two years have gone by and our US citizens are still waiting for that help to arrive. Spike Lee did a documentary called "When the Levees Broke: A

Requiem in Four Acts," this documentary shows you footage and talks to survivors that give you an actual account of what they went thru, what they actually saw, and what is exactly going on a year later and how their lives have been affected by Hurricane Katrina. Once again I know this may seem trivial to some people but can you look at this as well these are majority African Americans and other minorities having to deal with this and the President of the United States and the federal government are just going to keep pointing fingers at each other saying we are going to help and we will do what ever it takes, or can we just say that because of the deadlines and ultimatums that our fellow US citizens in need are just going to have to wait until our government gets ready to do something. Ok let me give you something else to think about, going back to what you read early about favoritism, racism what category do you think the survivors of Hurricane Katrina would fall under? This is a subject that can be talked about and debated on and on forever until more positive things happen in this region of the country to help our people out so, to the White House and the federal government what are you prepared to do and how long is it going to take before you decide to do it?

I want to get back to the fact that Diversity, Values, Professionalism, or Favoritism, Racism in some cases does exist at work, is there any, you decide for yourself. As an African American or another minority when you go to work how tough is it to have to deal with favoritism, racism and the threats of being written up for not doing what you are suppose to be doing? How tough is it when you want to learn as much as you can about the job that you are doing by coming to work early, staying late, and asking questions that will help you better understand what you are doing and management ignores you because of the color of your skin, or basically because you are not white? How tough is it when you apply for a position in management, and you have the experience in the job, you have taken some classes at your job to help better yourself and it means nothing because you're not white? How tough is it when you decide to go to college to get a degree and when you finish, you have your degree, you have the time on the job, you have the experience in the job, you have taken classes at your job and now, the education and the experience that you have you would think that this would be enough for you so the next time you apply for a position in management your chances of getting that position would be even greater now than before. You would think that all of this would make a difference but in reality it doesn't, that's because the person or persons that are in charge and make the decision about who or who not to promote is left in their hands and they are going to promote who ever they want to in the position that they want to put them in for as long as they can get away with doing it, and in a majority in most cases this person or persons are white. In some companies a case can be made that a job or jobs are made up so certain people can be placed in these jobs to give them a spot in management and in a majority of these cases the person just happens to be white. So once again I say to you is this Diversity, Values, Professionalism or Favoritism, Racism. If you ask most white people, they will say it's because they are qualified, and it's Diversity Values, Professionalism, if you ask most African Americans and other minorities, they will say its Favoritism, Racism.

As I stated earlier in this book, I've done some research about the structure of some companies and how the people in charge that make the decisions that affect the health and welfare and ultimately in some cases the way of life that some of their employees are trying to live. At the time that I was doing my research all of these companies and you will be reading about them shortly is set up pretty much the same way, predominately white and predominately male individuals are in charge so, you can draw your own conclusions. These are all well known companies, they have been in existence for a long time and not only that as an outsider looking in it just makes me wonder is this the norm of how businesses, companies or organizations which ever word you want to use is organized, they just keep going on without skipping a beat, business as usual no one is going to pay attention. I know this is a lot to digest but shouldn't we as African Americans and other minorities be aware of what is happening on our jobs and even at other large well known companies because in some way, shape or form this type of thinking may have an affect some kind of way on us at our jobs and just in our everyday lives in general.

First of all, let's take a look at Chevron Oil Company which is one of the largest integrated energy companies in the world and engaged in every aspect of the oil and natural gas industry. Chevron is a global enterprise that is highly competitive across all energy sectors. They also bring together a wealth of talent, shared values and a strong commitment to developing vital energy resources worldwide. This company aims to set the standard for the goals they achieve and how they achieve them. This company also says that their underlying values define who they are. Chevron as a company also talks about the fact that they make a commitment to value the talent of each individual, having the strengths of a diverse work force, and respecting and learning from the communities in which they operate. Finally, this company wants everyone to know that for them to remain successful; they demand the highest standards of social, economic and environmental responsibilities across their operations worldwide.

What they are trying to do is fine and dandy but my point is, as far as the leadership role of this company is concerned their makeup at the top is predominately white and male. These are the people that run the company *The Board of Directors Office of the Chairman/Chairman & Chief Executive Officer next, Vice Chairman of the Board after that there is an Executive Vice President Technology and Services, an Executive Vice President Upstream and Gas, an Executive Vice President Global Downstream, after that there is a Vice President Business Development, a Vice President General Counsel, a Vice President Chief Financial Officer, a Vice President Chief Technology Officer, a Vice President of Health, Environment and Safety, a Vice President and Chevron Global Gas, a Vice President and Comptroller, a Vice President and Treasurer, a Vice President and Chevron International Exploration & Production President, a Vice President Strategic Planning, a Vice President Human Resources, a Vice President and Chevron North America Exploration & Production President, a Vice President Policy Government and Public Affairs, and finally, there is a Corporate Secretary and a General Tax Counsel* so as you can see, a lot of people in charge to tell a lot of other people in charge what to do. Now, let me ask you this question, are these the best people for these jobs because of Diversity, Values, Professionalism and they have the education, qualifications, and skills or is it Favoritism, Racism because this company feels as though there aren't enough African Americans or other minorities that have the education, qualifications, or skills to do these jobs that are asked to be done?

Another oil company I'd like to tell you a little about is Exxon Mobil, and it too is also well known around the country. This company is committed to being the world's premier petroleum and petrochemical company. They continue to achieve superior financial and operating results while adhering to the highest standards of business conduct. Their success depends on the ability to consistently satisfy ever changing customer preferences. They pledge to be innovative and responsive with offering high quality products and services at competitive prices. The quality of this company's workforce is valuable and competitive. They strive to hire and retain the most qualified people available and maximize their opportunities for success through training and development. This company is committed to maintaining a safe work environment enriched by diversity and characterized by open communication, trust, and fair treatment. In the communities where they have their businesses, they pledge to be a good corporate citizen. They want to maintain the highest ethical standards, obey all laws and regulations, and respect local and national cultures. Basically the objective is to dedicate their business to running a safe and environmentally responsible operation. Here are the titles of the people at the top of this company, *Chairman and Chief Executive Officer of Exxon Mobil Corporation, Senior Vice President of Exxon Mobil Corporation, another Senior Vice President of Exxon Mobil Corporation, and yet another Senior Vice President and also Treasure of Exxon Mobil Corporation. This company also has a Board of Directors which is made up of twelve predominately white and male members* these men are in their fifties, sixties, and seventies and they to have input on some of the ways this company is being operated. Once again my question is, how can Exxon Mobil Corporation talk about having diversity and being fair and bias and not only that what they are trying to accomplish with their employees and the communities they have businesses in, when the people at the top who make the decisions are pretty much all predominately white and male?

Take a look at The Home Depot another company I'm going to tell you a little about because they are well known and do a lot of business in our communities as well. The Home Depot wants to be the best corporate partner possible in communities through positive contributions as a neighbor, an employer, and a retailer. This company also wants to help people to fulfill their dreams by helping them to live in a clean, safe and caring community, to be a part of a challenging, diverse, and inclusive workplace, and to create wealth and financial security. The Home Depot also wants to be the employer of choice because they say that their company provides meaningful and challenging work with the

opportunity for growth and development. They also want their potential employees to know that they strive to provide economic competitive wages and an exceptional benefits package. The Home Depot
wants everyone to know that they are dedicated to their values of taking
care of their people, giving back to the communities their stores are in
and to society as well, doing the right thing, providing excellent customer service, creating shareholder value, building strong relationships
and having good entrepreneurial spirit. All of that really sounds just a
little too good to be true, and I'm not saying that it's not true but, if
you ask some people in some of the communities that these stores are in
you might just get a different response. Remember the old saying that
"if it's too good to be true it's too good to be true," I just want to give
you something to think about. When you read about a company that
makes it seem like this is the place you want to be working, and don't
get me wrong this just might be where you want to work at after reading what they offer but, remember and think first, is this going to be a
dream job for me. Now let me tell you about the leadership of the
Home Depot, they have a *Chairman and CEO, next there is an Executive Vice President, Human Resources, Chief Operating Officer and Executive Vice President, Executive Vice President and Chief Information
Officer, Vice President-Secretary and Acting General Counsel, Chief
Financial Officer and Executive Vice President-Corporate Services to continue with the top leadership there is a Senior Vice President and Chief
Marketing Officer, Senior Vice President-Investor Relations, President-
Northern Division, Senior Vice President-Merchandising, President-EXPO
and Western Division, President-Southern Division, President-Mexico,
Senior Vice President-Corporate Communications and External Affairs
and President-The Home Depot Canada and Asia.* This is a lot of people
in charge, predominately white and male, telling their employees who

are majority African American and other minorities that work at this store, what they want done, how to do it and the beat goes on as usual.

Here's another example of a company that is well known nationally and internationally by not only the corporate world but the everyday consumer as well, Delta Air Lines. This company is America's fastest growing international carrier with more than 50 new international routes added in the last year. Their commitment to the community is to continuously create value through an inclusive culture by leveraging partnerships and servicing communities where they live and work, and they also strive to provide a hands on approach to recognizing every day that sometimes it takes more than an airplane to help lift someone off the ground. Delta Air Lines has a Code of Ethics and a Business Conduct which speaks for its' self and that is the Vision, Ethical Principles and Actions which are, to be the world's greatest airline, act with integrity, earn the trust of their stakeholders, respect and support each other, be loyal, act in a way the airline can be proud of and listen also, know what's right, do what's right, if you are ever unsure, ask, and keep asking until you get an answer. These are the corporate officers for this company and they stand behind and believe in what this company stands for because if they didn't, they wouldn't be in the positions that they hold. First there's *The Chief Executive Officer, Chief Operating Officer, Executive Vice President and Chief Financial Officer, Executive Vice President, Human Resources and Labor Relations, Executive Vice President and Chief of Network and Revenue Management, Executive Vice President and General Counsel, Executive Vice President Operations and finally, an Executive Vice President of Sales and Customer Service.* Guess what, here is another company run by predominately white and male individuals telling once again a majority of African Americans and other minorities, we want this done this way and if you do it you can keep your job. I may not be saying or putting the words in the right way or the way that some readers would like to see it but, so far what I've been saying about these companies politically correct or not ask yourself this question, what other words or phrases would you use or say to describe the top executives, the positions that they hold in these companies, and the oh by the way message that is telling African Americans and other minorities how they really feel about their management skills.

Here's another company that is large and well known, IBM. Now this company helped pioneer information technology over the years and it stands today at the forefront of a worldwide industry that revolutionizing the way in which enterprises, organizations and people operate and thrive. The character and the stamp that this company puts on its products, services and the marketplace is shaped and defined over time, it is expressed in an ever changing corporate culture in transformational strategies, and in new and compelling offerings for customers, nearly all of the company's products were designed and developed to record, process, communicate, store and retrieve information. IBM's values shape everything they do, and every choice they make on behalf of this company but, their real influence occurs when they apply these values to their personal work and their interactions with one another and world wide. This company is driven by these values: dedication to every client's success, innovation that matters for their company and for the world, and trust and personal responsibility in all relationships. Basically the business model for IBM is built to support two principal goals: helping their clients succeed in delivering business value by becoming more efficient and competitive through the use of business insight and information technology solutions, and providing long-term value to their shareholders, also inherent in this model is a commitment to employees and the communities in which they operate. Ok lets take a look at the corporate officers of this company first of all, *The Chair-*

man of the Board, President and Chief Executive Officer, next Chief Operating Officer in charge of Operations, Sales and Customer Service, Network and Revenue Management, Marketing, and Corporate Strategy, an Executive Vice President and Chief Financial Officer, an Executive Vice President, Human Resources and Labor Relations, an Executive Vice President and Chief of Network and Revenue Management, an Executive Vice President and General Counsel, an Executive Vice President Operations in charge of Technical Operations, Operations Control Center, Safety, Security, Airport Customer Service, COM air, Inc., Delta Connection Academy, and Delta air Elite, an Executive Vice President of Sales and Customer Service. Once again as you've just read this is a lot of people in charge telling a lot of other people in charge what to do and how to do it and once again repeating myself all of these corporate officers are predominately white and predominately male. As you have read so far there's not much difference in these companies and their corporate officers and basically who's at the top and who's not.

Staple's is another company I want to say something about and for your information if you don't know, they invented the office superstore concept and today are the world's largest office products company. Staples is committed to making it easy to buy a wide range of office products, serving consumers and businesses ranging from home-based businesses to Fortune 500 companies in 21 countries throughout North and South America, Europe and Asia. This company recognizes the close connection of financial success and a desire to make a positive impact on their associates, communities, and the planet by joining together diversity, the environment, their community, and ethics. Look at the corporate officers for this company, first *The Chairman and Chief Executive Officer next, President, North American Delivery a Senior Vice President, Corporate Controller, a Vice Chairman & Chief Financial Officer, a President & Chief Operating Officer, a President, U.S. Retail, an Executive Vice President, General Counsel and a Corporate Secretary, after all of these Executives there are even more under the title of Directors: Retired Vice Chairman, Staples, Inc, Chairman and Chief Executive Officer, Sara Lee Corporation, Owner and Chairman, Atlanta Falcons and Owner and Chairman, Georgia Force, Chairman and Chief Executive Officer, BB Capital, Inc., Executive Vice President and Chief Financial Officer, American Express Company, Chairman of the Board, Charles river Associates International, Chief Executive Officer, NAK Enterprises, L.L.C., Chairman and Chief Executive Officer, Staples, Inc., Chief Executive Officer, Samtex (USA), Inc. and Chairman and Chief Executive Officer, efunds Corporations.* This company too, predominately white and male individuals dominate the top spots and again tells the minority which is the majority of African Americans and other minorities employees, what and how they want their company run.

By now I know you have done a lot of reading and maybe even a lot of yawning but whether this is the case or not, I'm really trying to drive home the point to you that this is a serious issue and something that we as African Americans and other minorities can't just throw to the side and say it will take care of itself, let's just go on business as usual. We need to talk to as an individual and or even as a group to our front line managers and senior managers and stay on top of them, to let them know how we feel and some changes if any or not enough need to be made to keep our company running on an efficient bases or for that fact just to keep it in operation period.

Yet another company United Parcel Service or UPS as some people just say, is the world's largest package delivery company and a leading global provider of specialized transportation and logistics services, they also continue to develop the frontiers as they say, of logistics, supply chain management, and e-commerce combining the flows of goods, information, and funds. The workforce of UPS is multicultural, multidimensional, and reflective of the broad attributes of their global communities. UPS has been consecutively ranked by Fortune magazine as one of the "50 best companies for minorities." This company believes diversity is a valuable core component because it brings a wider range of resources, skills, and ideas to the business. UPS has found that over the years that they can not only grow by investing in their business but also in the communities where they live and work. Also as a company, UPS understands that customer diversity requires understanding the differences in cultural backgrounds and the unique needs of each customer. Ok, here is the makeup of the Board of Directors and get this, two of the same individuals are on the Board of Directors and the top management team. To start you have *The Chairman and Chief Executive Officer after that these are the other members, Chairman of the Board, Chief Executive Officer and President, Former Chairman and Chief Executive Officer, Former Chairman of the Board and Chief Executive Officer of Mark Controls Corporation, Chairman of the Board and CEO Symantec Corporation, Chief Executive, BT Group, Chief Financial Officer and Vice Chairman, Head of International Trade and Finance Covington & Burling, Executive Vice President, Technology Solutions Group, Hewlett-Packard Company, Senior Advisor, UBS Securities LLC, and Executive Vice President, Chief Financial Officer, the Home Depot.* As you can see by reading some of these Board Members work for other companies and at least two of them are former top executives brought in to be a part of this company. Now this is the top management at UPS first, *The Chairman and Chief Executive Officer, next to fall in line is the rest of top management starting with the Senior Vice President and Chief Information Officer, President, UPS International, Senior Vice President, Worldwide Sales and Marketing, Senior Vice President, Global Transportation Services, Senior Vice President, Supply Chain Group, Chief Operating Officer, UPS and President, UPS Airlines, Chief Financial Officer and Vice*

Chairman, Senior Vice President, Human Resources, Senior Vice President of Legal, Compliance and Public Affairs, General Counsel and Corporate Secretary, Senior Vice President, Communications and Brand Management and finally, Senior Vice President, U.S. Operations. These titles of the top management people of this company that you have just read are held by predominately white and male individuals, and once again these are the people making the decisions affecting the health and well-being and the lives in general of African Americans and other minorities that work for this company. Also here again ask yourself, if UPS wants to reflect themselves as a company that feels diversity is important and they want to show that to their employees and to the communities that their company's are in, why is it that the Board of Directors and the Top Management Group doesn't lead by example, why is it that the makeup of the Corporate Officers don't reflect diversity? It just seems to me like another old saying that goes "the pot calling the kettle black" if you know what I mean.

Another company I want you to look at, Verizon and they are one of the world's leading providers of communications services deploying fiber optics, broadband, wireless directory and data services. Verizon is one of the largest providers of wireline and wireless communications in the United States and internationally. As a company that serves millions of customers, it is imperative that they have an inclusive workforce. This company's definition of diversity includes the whole range of human differences, including age, ethnicity, education, sexual orientation, work style, race, gender and more. Over time, diversity has become an integral part of their business. Verizon firmly believes that embracing and cultivating diversity in their corporate culture is both the right business strategy and the right thing to do. This says that simply put, their goal is to operate their business with the highest level of integrity, responsibility and accountability and to continue to build on the trust that they have earned over the years. Ok take a look at the executive positions in this company, *Chairman and Chief Executive Officer Verizon Communications, Executive Vice President and General Counsel Verizon Communications, Executive Vice President and Chief Information Officer Verizon Communications, President and Chief Executive Officer Verizon Wireless, Vice Chairman and President Verizon Communications, Executive Vice President Strategy, Development and Planning Verizon Communications President Verizon Business, President Verizon Services Corporation, Group President International Verizon Communitions, Executive Vice President Human Resources Verizon Communications, Executive Vice President and Chief Marketing Officer Verizon Communications, Executive Vice President Public Affairs, Policy and Communications Verizon Communications, Executive Vice President and Chief Operating Officer Verizon Wireless, President Verizon Telecom, President and Chief Oprating Officer Verizon Communications, and finally Executive Vice President and Chief Financial Officer Verizon Communications. Next, here are the Senior Leaders of this company, to start Senior Vice President Investor Relations Verizon Communications, Senior Vice President and Chief Marketing Officer Verizon Business, Senior Vice Presiedent and Chief Information Officer Verizon Business, Senior Vice President Technology Chief/Technology Officer Verizon Communications, Senior Vice President Product Marketing Verizon Telecom and more, Executive Vice President Network Operations and Technology Verizon Business, Executive Vice President and Chief Marketing Officer Verizon Communications, Vice President Programming and Marketing Verizon FiOS TV, Executive Vice President of Enineering and Technology Verizon Telecom Group, Executive Vice President& Chief Technical Officer Verizon Wireless, Vice President and Chief Marketing Officer Verizon Wireless and finally, Chief Marking Officer Verizon Telecom.*

Once again it just amazes me that here is another company that talks about making progress through diversity, saying that diversity and inclusion are a critical link to their customers and communities, and also saying that embracing and cultivating diversity in their corporate culture is the right thing to do, than why is it that their executives and senior leaders don't reflect that, why is it that the individuals that make the decisions about how this company is going to run is predominately white and male? Everything that Verizon is saying they want to do sounds good but you mean to tell me that there aren't any qualified African Americans or other minorities besides the few that they have in these top level positions that can do the jobs that are being done, or is it that they feel as though there aren't any qualified African Americans or other minorities that can do the work that they are asking to be done, favoritism or racism ask yourself that question?

Another company and believe it or not, this company has the reputation of being one of the most popular information sources in business and informs people about local, national and international news and entertainment when and where it is happening on a daily basis in the U. S. and around the world, I'm talking about the New York Times. This company strives to leverage their brands across multiple media platforms, to the benefit their readers, advertisers, and employees. The New York Times Company is a leading media company, they publish the New York Times, The International Herald Tribune, The Boston Globe and 15 other daily newspapers; owns nine network-affiliated television stations and two New York radio stations; and has approximately 35 web sites. This company says that social responsibility is at the root of every facet of their organization. The commitment to philanthropy and supporting our communities is inspired by their history, business and employees and they support cultural, educational, community service, journalistic and environmental organizations. This company also focuses on programs addressing areas that a news organization can uniquely affect literacy and issues which are immediate concern to the communities, they are also committed to educational efforts including use of their newspapers as a learning tool.

Let me show you the make up of this company, *The Board Members consist of Ten Directors, then there is a Vice Chairman, The New York Times Company Publisher, International Herald Tribune next, President and Chief Executive Officer, The New York Times Company finally, Chairman, The New York Times Company Publisher, The New York Times.* Take a look at the Executives of this company and as you will see it is a lot of them starting with, *The Chairman, The New York Times Company Publisher, The New York Times,* after that all of these other company executives fall in line, *The President and Chief Executive Officer, Vice Chairman, The New York Times Company Publisher, International Herald Tribune, Senior Vice President and Chief Financial Officer, Senior Vice President, Corporate Development, Senior Vice President, Digital Operations, Senior Vice President, Human Resources, Senior Vice President, Process Engineering, Vice President, Real Estate Development, Vice President and Treasurer the New York Times Company, Vice President and Corporate Controller, Vice President, Internal Audit, Vice President, Diversity & Inclusion, Vice President, Organization Capability, Vice President, Forest Products, Vice President, Enterprise Services, Vice President, Compensation and Benefits, Vice President, Corporate Communications, Vice President and General Counsel, Vice President and Chief Information Officer The New York Times Company and Senior Vice President and Chief Information Officer The New York Times, Vice President, Research and Development Operations, Secretary and Corporate Governance Officer and finally, Assistant Treasurer.*

The New York Times has a Media Group of Executives as well that is in charge of the other media company's affiliated with The New York

Times Company. These are the company's and titles of the executives in charge starting with *The New York Times, President and General Manager, Executive Editor, Editor, Editorial Page, International Herald Tribune, Publisher, Executive Editor, Editor, Editorial Page, New England Media Group, Publisher, The Boston Globe, Editor, Editor, Editorial Page, Regional Media Group, President and Chief Operating Officer Regional Group and finally, Broadcast Media Group, President, Broadcast Media Group.*

These are a lot of people in positions of authority in this company and guess what the majority of them are predominately white and male and I'm thinking while writing this that African Americans or other minorities that work for this company just don't have enough time on the job or not enough experience to work in any of those positions or just don't have the education, qualifications or skills that the person or persons in charge are looking for to do these jobs, what do you think? Don't get me wrong there are a few minorities in authoritative positions with this company but, for the enormous size of The New Times and it's affiliates do you really think it could be a lot more than what it is or is it that the company is satisfied with the minorities they already have in certain positions.

Finally, the last company I want to tell you about is the Washington Post, and they are dedicated to top-quality journalism that is important to everyone at the company, including those who don't have a direct role in reporting or editing the news. Over the years the company's leaders have taken great risk to ensure that citizens have unfettered access to the news. Everyday, journalist at The Post, Post Newsweek television stations, Newsweek, Washingtonpost.Newsweek Interactive, The Gazette newspapers and their other news operations do everything possible and necessary to provide complete, fair and accurate news. This company takes pride in the high student and customer satisfaction ratings achieved by their education and cable divisions as they do in the journalism prizes won by their news organizations, they just want to be leaders in every field that they operate in. This company wants to grow even more by creating new businesses, attracting more customers to their exiting publications and services, and operating more efficiently. To achieve these goals they encourage an entrepreneurial spirit, a willingness to take risk and a realization that not every venture is going to succeed, and above all, they want to continue to build the essential value of the company. The goals of the Washington Post are: to produce the best newspapers, magazines, television programs, educational services and other products they can, to run an out standing business, to be not just a good, but an exceptional place for people to work, and a leader in the hiring and promotion of minorities and woman, to be a company that provides outstanding customer service, to be creative, adaptive, flexible and intelligent enough to adapt to the changes in our business environment, and to be a respected part of the communities where they do business.

These are the leaders of the Washington Post and their mission is to create a life changing forum that empowers individuals and build tremendous responsibility which requires the work of dedicated and talented people, all of whom work everyday reality. To start, *The Chief Executive Officer and Publisher, Executive Editor, Managing Editor for Multimedia, Vice President Marketing Washingtonpost.Newsweek Interactive, Vice President Business Development and General Counsel, Chief Operating Officer, Vice President Advertising Sales, Vice President of Sales Development and Operations Manager of Newsweek and Budget Travel Washingtonpost.Newsweek Interactive, Vice President of Classifields and Local Products, Vice President of Technology, Vice President of Product Development, Vice President and Editor-in-Chief of New Ventures Washingtonpost.Newsweek Interactive.*

Here we go again, this is a lot of people in charge telling a lot of other people in charge telling the employees what they want and how they want it done, and finally just to go out and do it. Ok how about this, the people in charge are predominately white and male and once again the African Americans and other minorities that work for this company have to abide by and comply with what they are told to do.

I can't speak for any of the employees of any of these companies that I have just written about but, I'm pretty sure that there are issues going on that they have to deal with everyday they go to work and even though they may agree or disagree with what is happening they still do their jobs in a professional way and when issues do arise they are taken care of in an appropriate manner.

I know after reading this portion of the book you might be saying to yourself what's going on with these companies, do they really need these many people to tell another bunch of people what to do and how to do it or, is this just some job titles that were made up by whom ever owns these companies to give some people a position of authority who knows maybe or maybe not. Once again as you can see African Americans and other minorities get the short end of the stick because predominately white and male men are in charge and making the decisions that the employees have to go by.

There are other issues that I would like to talk briefly about and politics is the first one. The position of President of the United States, and at the time that I'm writing this book our President is George W. Bush. Why is it that the few African Americans that have made the attempt to run for this office and let's look at some of the names, Shirley Chisholm, Jesse Jackson Sr., Al Sharpton and Carol Moseley-Braum, have never been voted into this position or for that fact even Vice-President of the United States. Is it that these African Americans were not qualified for either one of these positions, as registered voters of the United

States are some of us just so use to seeing a white male as President and didn't want to vote for them, or how about some of us just don't have enough confidence to vote for an African American? The statements that I made at the beginning of this book talking about diversity, values, professionalism or is it favoritism, racism do you think we can put this in one of those categories? Let's continue to look at this, some people won't vote for an African American or other minority as President of the United States because in some cases the color of their skin, because of the backgrounds they come from, the schools that they may or may not have attended or, just because some of the people that they associate with, there could be so many reasons so this list could go on and on for ever so think about it, is it Favoritism, Racism?

The United States Senate is another issue to briefly take a look at because once again the make up of the Senate is predominately male, predominately white and check this out over the years in my life time besides former Senators Edward William Brooke, III and Carol Moseley-Braun who was the first African American woman to become a U.S. Senator and now present Senator Barack Obama have been and are now African American members of the house of Senate. Here's a Black History Fact for you to remember "did you know" that there were two other African American Senators, Hiram Revels of Mississippi was the first Black Senator in 1870 and five years later also from Mississippi Blanche K. Bruce was sworn into this office. So, here we go again are these predominately white males voted into office because they are the best men qualified for the position or do some voters want and feel as though there are no qualified African American men or women that can do the job that needs to be done in the Senate? Well can we say that this is diversity, values, professionalism because this is what some voters want and feel or is this favoritism, racism because this is what some voters want or feel? So what do you think and how do you feel about the makeup of the United States Senate draw your own conclusions?

Next, how about the highest court in the land, the Supreme Court and ask yourself, out of all of the African American male and female lawyers, judges, district and state attorneys that there are here in the United States over the years the former Presidents and the current President that is in office now, you mean to tell me that besides former Justice Thurgood Marshall and present Justice Clarence Thomas there are no qualified African American men or women that can sit on the Supreme Court. Think about it and ask yourself name two more or just one more African American that I may have overlooked that had in the past a seat on the Supreme Court? In this case this is not a question of what some voters want or feel about a person that should be in this position of authority but, this is a question that the President of the United States makes and he feels as though there aren't any African American men or women best qualified to sit on the Supreme Court. Ok, is this a decision made by the President using diversity, values, professionalism to make sure that the right person or, the best qualified person is in this position or, is this favoritism, racism because the former Presidents and the current President just don't want an African American besides the former one and the current one to sit on the Supreme Court, once again ask yourself and draw your own conclusions?

There are a lot of other political issues that can be discussed and I'm pretty sure that after reading some of these you may have a lot that you could talk about as well, and to be honest with you I can just imagine your brain waves are racing at the speed of light and thoughts are just popping in and out of your mind but I did say briefly talk about so let me move on.

I want to talk a little bit about higher education and I' referring to colleges and universities. Something that's always been on my mind schools like Harvard, Yale, Brown, Cornell, and other ivy league schools are perceived by some people as being top flight, the cream of the crop and any other phrase that you can think of but basically these are the schools that make an individual stand out when applying for a job in the work force. On the other hand Historically Black Colleges and Universities like Howard, North Carolina Central, Florida A&M, Morgan State, and other HBCUS in some peoples minds just don't stand out as much for an individual applying for a job in the work force. It shouldn't make a difference what college or university a person decides to go to and further their education because the more knowledge you have the better chances you have or I should say the better chances you are suppose to have of getting into and making the type of career opportunities for yourself. Once again this is a stumbling block for some African Americans and even other minorities because at times we get slapped in the face trying to make a career move and it becomes an up hill battle and takes us an even longer time to get to the top than it should all because of the color of our skin or who we are and the college or university we decided to go to. Let's be real in a majority of cases we as a minority in a lot of instances can't afford to pay for an education at an ivy league school or for that matter at times we really can't afford to pay for an education at any school but, sometimes because of the grace of God we are fortunate enough to find a way so we can go to school and continue our education if we want to. Think about it, the stereotype that's given to people attending certain schools and having the advantage of obtaining a job that's considered to be let's say more prestigious than another, and all I'm saying is, attending an ivy league school over an HBCU, do you think in this case ivy league schools teach or stress certain things more than others or, it's just difficult to get into these schools because of academics or, do you think this could possibly fall into the category of favoritism, racism? There are so many other reasons why getting into some schools are more difficult than others and I could have used an example other than that of ivy league schools but whether it's Ohio State, UCLA, Kentucky or for that matter North Carolina in some peoples minds schools that are HBCUS for some reason or another are not considered as prestigious in the academic world and in some cases as I stated early when applying for jobs in the work force that same stereotype often at times stays with a graduate from an HBCU. This is one of those topics that can be talked about forever and as an African American it's tough when even higher education along with trying to get a job once obtaining a degree is difficult as well so lets be honest, the struggle continues after college and we can never ever give up to get what we want.

So far I've been talking about businesses and how they are majority owned and operated by predominately white and male individuals and how they make the decisions that affect the lives and well being of their employees which in a majority of cases is African Americans and other minorities. Higher education and I mean colleges and universities and how they are perceived by some employers and in a majority of most cases the employers that make the decisions about who to hire or not are predominately white and male so, just because of the name of the school their potential employee or employees attended or didn't attend and in most cases because of this African Americans or other minorities are a majority of the times on the outside looking in. Politics and the President of the United States, the make up of his cabinet, and the United States House of Senate how it is structured and in both cases, the President who has always been white and male and the majority of his cabinet too has always been predominately white and male, the Senators on the other hand haven't been any different, besides the names of the African Americans that I mentioned the majority of Senators have been predominately white and male and just remember these are the people that make the decisions that not only affect the health, lives and well being of African Americans and other minorities but every citizen here in the United States as well.

Now I want to talk about something that I'm a big fan of, that's professional sports and I'm going to single out three that I think are talked about more than others and to me even though it is just a game I think these sports are so exciting at times I just can't get enough of them. Major League Baseball, the National Football League, and the National Basketball Association, all three of these sports are dominated by African Americans and other minorities and the salaries of these players and the benefits that they receive are astronomical. On the playing fields and in the arenas where these athletes perform hundreds of thousands of fans come out to see them, cheer them on and in some cases boo them if the players do or say something that the fans don't like. Before the games are played there are a lot of behind the scene activity that take place and that's the business side of professional sports. The business part is what I want to talk about and the make up of the front offices and how they operate. Major League Baseball has a league office and thirty teams that are set up in different cities across the United States and each team has offices as well. The National Football League has its league office and thirty two teams that are set up in different cities across the United States and each team has offices as well. The National Basketball Association also has a league office and thirty teams that are set up in different cities across the United States and each team has offices as well. The owners of these sports franchises are predominately white and male, the person in charge of each of the leagues is predominately white and male, and the person that pretty much runs the front office for the individual teams is predominately white and male as well. There are a few exceptions to this as far as ownership of a team and running the front office is concerned but still it's nothing compared to the overall picture and how one group of individuals is basically in charge. The thing we have to look at here is these are white men that how ever they did it basically have a lot of money, had the motivation, influence, and guts enough to take the chance to buy a sports franchise. Now can we fault them for running their business, and these owners are really running a business the way they want to do it or, can we as African Americans and other minorities try and influence them to give these athletes an opportunity to show and prove to these owners that after their playing days are over to give them a chance to be a part of their business off the field. In a lot of cases these athletes do go to school and study business, they do have ideas about how a business can and should be run and just like everyone else if they make a mistake they can correct it and move on to keep things running just as smooth as they were before. Can it be said that the owners pick and choose, which they do and have the right to, who they want to run their team and also decide and if I didn't say this before, the owners decide who will be the person in charge of their professional sports league so, as I've been talking about throughout this book, is this done using the first category I mentioned diversity, values, professionalism by choosing the person that knows and understands what it takes to operate and keep the particular league and the front office they are in charge of running smooth or basically is this the best qualified person or, can their choice be put in the second category I mentioned favoritism, racism because the particular individual that is chosen is liked by all of the owners and that's who they want to be the head of their league and that's who they want to run their office or, is it because the individual is white and male and they just don't want an African American or any other minority to be in charge of their business period, draw your own conclusion?

I've talked to a lot of African Americans and other minorities not only on my job but other jobs in and around the Washington, D. C. area about some general concerns and issues that I feel revolves around the topic of what I'm writing about which is Diversity, Values, Professionalism, or Favoritism, Racism: African Americans and Other Minorities In The Work Force. The one thing that I want all of my readers to know is that the people that I talked to on my job and people that work at other places of employment didn't want me to use their name or the place that they work at because of fear of some type of retaliation from their employers. I want everyone to remember this, even though it is not suppose to happen believe it or not when people talk about issues going on at their job that may be detrimental, retaliation of some sort does happen and in most cases the employee that does the talking is the one that takes the brunt of the negative backlash.

I'd like to talk to you about some of the experiences that I and other minorities are going through on my present job and how it relates to this topic. As I stated near the beginning of this book I live in the suburbs surrounding Washington, D.C. and fortunate enough for me, I was able to get a job with one of I think the best companies in this area. Let me just start off by saying, I'm not going to mention the name of the company, the name of the person in charge or the people that are in positions of authority. Now don't get me wrong this is a good company that I work for, I work around and work with a lot of good people and the benefits that are provided to take care of me and my family is good. My purpose is to tell you about how I've been affected and at times other minorities as well and what we are dealing with everyday as we go to work to try to make a living for ourselves and our families so, as I've been saying throughout this book you draw your own conclusions, is this diversity, values, professionalism, or favoritism, racism.

On June 3, 1985 after taking a test and a physical for the position that I wanted and at the time this was required before getting a job with this company, I starting working on this day. I began the day signing a lot of papers in personnel and then different representatives from departments talked to me and other new employees about some of the do's and don'ts, what is expected as an employee, and some of the history as well, basically this was my orientation into the company. Years and years had gone by in my life and I had been trying to get a job at this company for the longest time but I could just never get in, lucky for me with help from a friend of mind at the time, I got the opportunity, took advantage of it and what can I tell you, as that old saying goes, "the rest is history."

My first job allowed me to work around some very good people and to be in this type of atmosphere was just great. Ok, starting out I worked in a department that required me to guard and protect fellow employees and their property and other property that belongs to this company. Guest and visitors that were allowed and or came onto the property of this company, it was my job to guard and protect them and their property and assist them in what ever way I could as well. I liked what I was doing it was rewarding and kept me moving around a lot but after a while I just wanted to do something else. After working in this department for about eight months I starting looking at the in-house job announcements to see if there was any other type of work I could do that was a little more challenging, gave me a little more responsibility, and of course a pay increase as well. The search came to an end when I found another job that I liked and lucky enough for me I was interviewed and got the job.

The second position that I moved on to in this company was in the administration field and unlike the previous position that I had where I moved around a lot, this job required me to work at one specific location everyday in an office type of atmosphere. Like I said before I liked my previous job a lot, I just wanted to do something else. This new job that I moved into required me to do a lot of paperwork, assist other employees with their jobs at times when it was necessary, answer telephones and write down repair or replacement orders from other employees and input those orders into a computer, and afterwards make sure that the proper departments were notified to take care of those repair or replacement orders. At times this job got to be a little demanding but, I liked doing it and I liked the challenge it gave me and not only that, it allowed me the opportunity to show my supervisor that the right decision was made when I got hired for this job. I know this might sound funny but at this time in my life I kind of got board with working in an office type of atmosphere and just wanted to do something else so, after about seven months on this job I once again starting looking at the in-house job announcements to see if there was something else in this company that I could do. Now of course with moving along to another job I want to have some responsibility and increase my pay status as well so that was the objective that I had in mind. After searching and searching the in-house job announcements, the responsibility, and of course the money that I was looking for came along. At that time the pay increase for me was a very big jump from what I was getting before so I was more than happy to make that move.

The department that I moved into this time was very demanding somewhat like the previous one but just like the previous one, I was prepared to meet the challenge head on and do the job to the best of my ability. Starting out my responsibilities required me to assist other employees in the performance of their jobs, which was maintenance and repair work and at times was of a difficult nature. The work that I was doing was important because the general public counts on the services that this company I work for provides because without maintenance and repair work and other up keep that needs to be done on this job, not only would some of the general public but some of the other employees of this company as well would find it difficult to get to and do their everyday jobs. I did this type of work in this section of this department for four years, unfortunately it took me that long to decide that I wanted to do something more than assist other employees doing their jobs, I wanted to do some work that I was responsible for and ultimately have employees that I could show them, teach them, and eventually they would be accountable to me about the work that they are doing. In order for me to advance and try to do this I took a promotional test and passed after which I moved into another section, still in this same department hoping that this would start me on that road that I wanted to be a part of.

I became a maintenance mechanic, now this job required me to do basic repairs on structures that were made of concrete, by this I mean stop or divert water leaks, remove and repair bad concrete, inspect and write reports on buildings and other concrete structures. This job also required me to do other things such as fence repair, operate heavy equipment and at times do repair or inspection work that needs to be done, and to also escort employees that do not work for this company on to the property in certain restricted areas so they can do what ever job the company is paying them to do as well. I not only did the physical labor work but after a while, I was asked by management to take a group of men out on a job site to do maintenance work, be responsible for not only my safety but the safety of the men as well, and then after all of the work was done submit a report to management explaining exactly what the men and I did and whether or not the job was completed. Also on several occasions management asked me to act in the position of management which required me to do a lot of administrative paper work, a lot of other administrative duties, and not only that once again I was responsible for my safety and the safety of all of the employees that I was in charge of as well. All of the times that I acted in a management position, I was never told by anyone in charge that I didn't do a good job and in my opinion I thought that I handled the job well enough to keep everything running smooth, at least I thought I was. In my present position management is still asking me to take a group of men out on a job site and do some maintenance work but, as far as acting in the capacity of management is concerned or even after the number of times that I have applied for a position in management basically, I'm being told that I no longer have the education, qualifications or skills to be in an acting position as a manager. I say this because lately everyone that has been hired as a manager in this department that I work in has a lot less time in this company than I do, they don't have as much experience on this job as I do, and from what I personally know about some of them, their education, qualifications and skills don't compare to what I have accomplished. Another thing that bothers me is that a majority of the positions being filled in management are by predominately white males and in other instances if an employee is in good favor with the person in the position that makes the decision about who will get a position in management and in this case I mean the superintendent of the department, they are getting the management jobs as well. Let me just say that when I go to work I'm going to do my job, I'm going to do what ever I'm asked to do and I'm not going to create any issues. Another thing I'd like to say is, everyday when I go to work it frustrates me that all of the hard work that I have put into this job to gain a better understanding of it, and all of the years that I put a lot of time and effort in going back to school to get a degree to help better my opportunities on this job and in this company, it just seems like a slap in the face and a waste of time when I still have to struggle to get into a position in management that I know I can handle. Other African

Americans and other minorities have told me if not the same thing similar instances that they are going thru as well and they are just as frustrated as I am. Once again the person or persons in charge, the superintendents or department heads, that make the decisions on my job that affect not only me but other African Americans and other minorities as well and to that extent affect the education, health and well being are predominately white and predominately male. The decisions that are made ultimately gives me, other African Americans, and other minorities as well more options to advance even higher in our education because of the pay raises that come with a promotion, and not only that control in their hands whether or not we advance into the position of management. As I stated before it seems to me that instead of promoting people into management positions on my job using diversity, values and professionalism to make things equal and fair for every employee, favoritism and racism is taking place and because this has been going on for a period of time to me no one seems to care enough to do anything about it. I have personally talked to individuals in the department of EEOC on several occasions at my company and basically I've been told by them and have received personal correspondence in the mail that, after looking into my concerns and issues nothing out of the ordinary can be found to justify my concerns and issues. Like I said before when favoritism and racism and not diversity, values, professionalism is going on right in front of your face and the department of your company that you have asked to look into this matter is suppose to be the helping hand in making sure that these type of once again, concerns and issues are looked into, dealt with, and resolved so these and once again, type of concerns and issues won't continuously keep happening. The reason why I continue to stress my point about concerns and issues is because just like I have been stating throughout this book, how can these matters in reality really be eliminated when the individual or individuals in charge are predominately white and male. Someone that hasn't walked in your shoes, that hasn't had to deal with as a African American or other minority, just basically someone who has never had to deal with any type of discrimination at all, how can they explain to you or tell you how you are suppose to feel and then come back with this line of don't worry you'll be taken care of and everything is going to be alright, it just can't be done. So you tell me, after reading this book am I wrong for thinking favoritism, racism and not diversity, values, professionalism is a part of the work environment in general here in the United States, or should I just go on thinking that this is business as usual and hopefully with the laws that are already in place and with the new faces that we have on Capital Hill and in some local, state and federal government offices as well that changes will come along more sooner than later.

In conclusion, Diversity, Values, Professionalism or Favoritism, Racism African Americans and Other Minorities In The Work Force no matter how much we want to believe it or not does exist. As African Americans and other minorities at a young age this should be one of the many things taught in high school and reiterated in college so by the time as individuals they enter the work force, they are prepared for in some cases maybe not all, the type of attitude that can be expected from some employers. It's hard to explain sometimes especially to not all but some young people about different types of work environments and just basically life in general and that's why I stress the point that these are some of the things that should be taught to them at a young age. Whether you agree or disagree with what I'm saying, if you plant the seed early and keep it stable and in tact, it should grow and blossom into something that will amaze you, simply put, show and talk to kids and not only African Americans and other minorities but just kids in general while they are young and they should grow and turn into an adult to be proud of.

Minorities period have had to deal with in the past and unfortunately to this present day some form of favoritism or racism in the work force and in particular in their lives in general. In my life time African Americans to me seem to take the lead position of favoritism and racism because, as an African American male to some white individuals, I'm looked at as African American first and a man second. African American females really have it bad because to some white individuals, they are looked at as an African American first, female second and third a minority. To go even further minorities period unfortunately in a lot of cases for some reason or another are looked at by some white individuals as a minority first and a man or women second so, for these reasons that I've just mentioned and probably a lot more that can be thought of ask yourself, how can we as African Americans and other minorities on our jobs and just in our everyday lives can we be expected to be treated fair if predominately white and male individuals are in charge and make the decisions that affect our education, health, lives and well being.

I've talked about a lot of things and have tried to stress a lot of points in this book because I want to give you an abundance of my thoughts and opinions that I think should be talked about and get together as a united group and hopefully do something about them. Take these thoughts and spread them around to your family, friends, co-workers and just other people that you know and maybe one day as it has happened many times in the past we can become united as a group to make necessary changes in our lives to make things better for minorities in this country period.

Reference

To read for yourself and see more about if you don't already know, the President of the United States and his cabinet, the make up of the U. S. Senate, the African American Senators and their biographies that were in office before Edward William Brooke, III, Carol Moseley-Braum and Brack Obama, and of course the ten companies that I talked about, go to these web sites:

www.whitehouse.gov

www.senate.gov

Go to goggle and type in: *Hiram Rhodes Revels, Blanche Kelso the African American Senators*

www.chevron.com

www2.exxonmobil.com

www.delta.com

www-03.ibm.com

corporate.homedepot.com

www.staples.com

www.ups.com

multimedia.verizon.com

www.nytco.com

www.washpostco.com

Note: *I checked three web sites, amazon.com, goggle.com and yahoo.com because I wanted you to see photos and read names and biographies of members of the U.S. Supreme Court but, all you can do on these sites is read names and biographies. There should be a web site that has photos and biographies of these members although, after doing my research of a few sites I just don't know of and couldn't find one.*

978-0-595-47122-5
0-595-47122-6

www.ingramcontent.com/pod-product-compliance
Lightning Source LLC
Chambersburg PA
CBHW050335290526
45785CB00006B/2503